Praise for *Southern Fried Faith*

One of the biggest challenges for the church today is to see through the clutter of cultural Christianity to the unchanging, biblical gospel that creates a new kind of culture in its place. *Southern Fried Faith* is written by a pastor who loves the church in the South enough to affirm its beauty where possible and challenge its idolatry where needed. This is a funny, convicting, and hope-filled book.

Trevin Wax
Managing Editor of The Gospel Project at LifeWay Christian Resources
Author of *Gospel-Centered Teaching, Counterfeit Gospels, and Clear Winter Nights*

Having grown up in the American South where the "behavior modification program" too often passes for the authentic following of Jesus, Rob Tims brings very good tidings. For hopeless sinners like me, *Southern Fried Faith* is a welcome disruption and an invitation to freedom for believers from anywhere on the map.

Derek Webb
Artist and Entrepreneur

This book was written by a Southern-fried preacher, alright, but one who understands the priority of the gospel over its cultural encasement. There is nothing mean-spirited or angry in this volume, but much honest probing and candid exploration from one who has thought deeply about the joys and the discomforts of discipleship and ministry in the school of Jesus Christ.

Timothy George
Founding dean of Beeson Divinity School of Samford University
Chairman of the Board of the Colson Center for Christian Worldview

This book, *Southern Fried Faith,* aims to show that the church of the South can relate to the culture of the South without being absorbed by it. Pastor Tims writes so that the church of the South might be recognized by its allegiance to Christ rather than its attachment to the southern culture. This work is different in its perspective in order to make a difference in its impact.

Dr. Robert Smith
Professor ofChristian Preaching at Beeson Divinity School

It's been said that the gospel is a seed that grows in the soil of the culture. But what happens when we confuse the soil with the seed? This book addresses that issue not from the outside, but from inside the religious South, helping pastors and church leaders diagnose those cultural characteristics that so subtly and destructively into the minds and hearts of church members. Rob helps us see with biting insight as well as humor the distinctive challenge and calling it is to shepherd in the South.

Michael Kelley
Director of Discipleship at Lifeway
Author of *Boring* and *Wednesdays Were Pretty Normal*

Southern Fried Faith

How the Bible Belt Confuses Christ and Culture

Rob Tims

Published by Rainer Publishing
www.rainerpublishing.com

ISBN 978-0692210215

Printed in the United States of America

Contents

Acknowledgements

I am not afraid that the book will be controversial,
I'm afraid it will not be controversial.
— Flannery O'Connor

I am highly indebted to a number of people for this book. My wife, Holly, has been an unshakeable force of love and support, particularly in very hard years of ministry that have contributed greatly to the content of this book. My friends and coworkers at LifeWay Christian Resources (Michael Kelley, Laura Magness, and Brandon Hiltibidal, to name a few) have shared great wisdom, insight, and encouragement. Without them, I am a lesser steward of the experiences God has given me.

I also am thankful for Derek Webb, who spent two hours with me the day before Thanksgiving to talk about Jesus and the church and aid me in writing and promoting this book. I am grateful for the fine people at Rainer Publishing who took a chance on an obscure, barely-published author and served him well.

More than anyone else, I am grateful to the quintessential southern belle, my mom: Janet Garrison. Without her firm but gentle push to use the experiences, time, and other resources God has given me, this book doesn't exist. In the midst of her affliction, she continued to encourage and inspire.

Chapter 1

Lovin' Southern

"While the South is hardly Christ-centered, it is most certainly Christ-haunted."
- Flannery O'Connor

Growing up southern is a privilege. If you're from the South, you understand my sentiment. The food alone is enough to justify permanent residence: fried okra, white rice with butter and sugar, green beans sautéed in bacon grease left over from breakfast. The South has good food and great people.

I believe the nation's kindest, best-humored people are southerners. They will butter you up even as they butter your corn bread. Who would want to live anywhere else? Who would willingly choose to live north of the Mason-Dixon Line knowing what they could have south of it?

That's not to say that every part of the South is for every person in the South, or that all things southern are for all southerners. We have our differences. I recall taking my first road trip with my fiancé so she could meet my mother and stepfather. Somewhere along the way of that 6-hour drive, we pulled over for fuel and refreshments. I don't recall the drink I chose, but I do remember grabbing an old stand-by snack: a six-pack of miniature powdered donuts. I do not recall what snack my wife chose, but I do remember her drink: a Nehi grape soda.

"Grape soda?" I said. "You really are a redneck, aren't you?"

She pointed to my powdered donuts. "Who's the redneck?"

Powdered donuts and grape soda: a match made in heaven … or at least a match made in the South. Or is there even a difference?

After our visit, we drove to my hometown in the Mississippi Delta in order for friends and family to meet my soon-to-be bride. My hometown is a thriving metropolis of 8,000 or so, and is 115 miles directly south of Memphis, TN. The terrain is flat and fertile. There are no natural hills for miles in any direction, and very few trees. One cannot grow corn, soybeans, or cotton—and certainly cannot farm catfish—with hills and trees.

During this drive my fiancé gazed at the unimpressive landscape and said, "If I was not confident you loved me, I'd swear you were taking me somewhere to kill me so that no one could find me."

"You don't understand," I said. "The Delta is home to the most beautiful sunsets you will ever see."

"I don't envision our life including Delta sunsets," she replied.

That was fine with me. No one stays out to see the Delta sunsets anyway, especially in the summer, for fear of being carried away by mosquitoes.

We ended up marrying in the upstate of South Carolina, not far from her hometown of Gaffney. Gaffney is peach country, and the town is famous for an unusually large water tower that is shaped and painted to resemble the naked south end of a north-facing... I mean, a peach. I had about as much affection for Gaffney as she did for the Mississippi Delta, so we had to establish a new home as a new family.

Only in the South, of course. All things southern are not for all southerners, and we were willing to live anywhere, but we preferred to root, bloom, and produce fruit in the South. We desired to go to restaurants that served sweet tea. We wanted Yankees to be the ones with funny accents. We hoped to use phrases like "I used ta could" or "I am fixin' to do it" and not be questioned about our command of the English language.

We wanted to say "y'all" and not be mocked. We sought the surroundings of hospitable, hard-working, kind and patriotic people who usually did the right thing just because you're supposed to. We aspired to live where most people went to church on Sundays. We wanted to live in the American South. For most of our 13 years together, we have had this privilege.

It's been a bit of a redneck tour (Alabama, Texas, South Carolina, and Tennessee), and we deviated to the east coast of South Florida for a couple of years, but we have been blessed to live in the land we love, and we do not take it for granted.

That's not to say my love for the South is blind. I'm all too familiar with many of our problems. Among the most obvious is race. Many in the South struggle with the growing ethnic diversity in our country.

More subtly and perhaps just as pervasively, we in the South are a "feel good" kind of people, which is to say, if it feels good, we tend to do it. Southerners with stricter moral codes might avoid giving in to their emotions when it comes to something like alcohol or sex, but, by and large, our feelings tend to guide our decision making in ways that are frequently unhealthy. Simply using the phrase, "It felt like a good idea at the time" can cover a multitude of sins in the South.

Hospitality in the South is unrivaled. When I talk with Yankees who are on vacation or have just moved to the South, they almost always say, "Everyone is so nice." Of course we are. But they don't know what we may really be thinking. We may simply be keeping the peace, telling ourselves how much better we are than them so that we'll be nice to them and they will think highly of us.

If we've ever said, "Bless your heart" to you, we're glad you felt better about whatever stupid thing you did, but that was really our way of saying, "We're so much better than you! Aren't you thankful for how kindly we have expressed our superiority?"

Southerners are busy, hard-working people. Our accents may be lazy, but we use those as a ploy to catch others off guard and get ahead of them. The work ethic of most southerners is unparalleled. We take great pride in this, and as a result, we tend to look down on people who make it a habit to rest or relax. Making such sluggards feel guilty is a great way to motivate them into more work that benefits us and strokes our ego.

So while I love the South, I love it with eyes wide open. I willingly embrace it and immerse myself in it, fully aware of our troubles. That's what true love does, after all.

The Church in the South

Perhaps the thing I love most about the South is the church. The South isn't the South I love without the church. I grew up in the 1970s and 1980s when the church was still the center of social life, especially in small towns. School or athletic events on Wednesday nights, Sundays, or within a week of a Christian holiday were unheard of.

The community had great respect for the local church because the local church served the community well. The South just wouldn't be the

9

South we all know and love if it weren't for the church.

In those days, many parents in the South were of the opinion that, whether you liked it or not, you went to church. My parents were no exception, and for the most part, I loved it. I proudly wore the same khaki pants and blue button-down shirt to worship week in and week out. I loved children's choir on Sunday afternoons and Royal Ambassadors in the church basement on Wednesday nights.

I loved fried catfish supper fundraisers. I loved Sunday school at 9:15, "big church" at 11:00, youth choral ensemble at 3:30, youth choir at 4:30, snack supper at 5:45, youth Bible study at 6:00, and "night church" at 7:00 every Sunday. I loved youth hand bells, choir tours, shaving cream balloons, and lock-ins. I listened to Petra, 4Him, Out of the Grey, Point of Grace, and Steven Curtis Chapman. I could not get enough southern-style church, so much so that God called me to serve it for the rest of my life.

Despite my deep love, I'm not any less blind to the church in the South than I am the South at large. Let's face it: the church of the American South has her issues. She bears a striking resemblance to the first-century church in Ephesus. In Revelation

2:1-7, Jesus commended the Ephesians for battling hard against the moral decline of their surroundings and defending against doctrinal impurity. These are things the southern church does well.

There are few people groups that progressive liberals hold in contempt more than we who are fighting for America's soul in the South. We are heartbroken and angry at the loss of virtue we see taking place in our country. We are hard-working people who want the best for our children and grandchildren. We see the Bible and its Judeo-Christian ethic as foundational to a healthy society, and we are not about to simply let it slip away without a fight.

This is an admirable thing, but the great threat to such churches is that they fall in love with the work they do for God in place of God Himself. And God has nothing to do with such churches. Indeed, God would just as soon let a church full of hard-working, truth-loving, culture warriors dis-appear if they loved being that way more than they loved Him.

As Jesus said to the church in Ephesus, *"I will come to you and remove your lampstand from its place—unless you repent"* (Revelation 2:5).

In other ways, the southern church resembles the first body of believers in Laodicea. Jesus chastised that church for resembling its culture more than it resembled Him. In the same way that the Laodiceans found their identity in their community's wealth, the church in the South tends to find its identity in being "southern." Rather than resist the sinful tendencies of our culture, we tend to embrace them as part of our Christian personality.

In doing so, we essentially operate without Jesus in the same way the Laodiceans did. Jesus beckons the southern church the same way He called out to the Laodiceans: *"Listen! I stand at the door and knock. If anyone hears My voice and opens the door, I will come in to him and have dinner with him, and he with Me"* (Revelation 3:20).

Jesus had loving, straightforward messages for both of these churches. He urged the Ephesian church to do three things: remember Him, repent of their sin, and live accordingly. He called upon the Laodiceans to "open the door" and rekindle their relationship with Him. These same actions are called for today in churches across the American South, for we have grown comfortable with being southern more than being like Jesus.

How, precisely? This book is not meant to uncover the problem comprehensively. I will, however, begin with five of the biggest issues troubling the church in the South.

First, we have an inclination to trust our emotions to guide us in making key decisions, often ignoring the truth of Scripture. While feelings are crucial to our faith, they must not be what we place our faith in.

Second, we prefer peace keeping to peace making. We tend to avoid conflict all together or cave to whatever makes certain people happy or causes the least amount of turmoil. Keeping the peace is admirable, but making peace is biblical.

Third, we relish in our accomplishments more than Jesus' accomplishment. In our quest to love others and help people walk with Jesus, we fall in love with our efforts and become legalistic people. As a result, we judge others more than we love them. We separate ourselves from them rather than live life among them.

Fourth, we have made church about us. We've come to believe that God and His church revolve around us instead of us around Him. As a result, we resort to personal gratification and guilt manipulation to coerce one another to participate in the church and its mission.

Finally, we fight harder for our earthly citizenship than our heavenly citizenship. We have fallen in love with the virtues that make our country great, treasuring them more than the gospel that brings them to bear. Love of country is biblical, but not at the expense of allegiance to the Kingdom of God.

Early church history shows that the Ephesian and Laodicean churches did, indeed, remember, repent and act, restoring Jesus as their first love. The question before us southern Christians is whether we will follow in their footsteps.

Einstein's Wisdom

Albert Einstein is quoted as saying that if he had one hour to save the world, he would spend fifty-five minutes defining the problem and only five minutes finding the solution. Einstein believed that by taking most of our time to understand a problem, we often need far less time to solve it. He understood that the quality of the solutions we create to solve a given problem is usually in direct proportion to the quality of our understanding of a problem.

This book is written in alignment with Einstein's premise. I do not pretend to have all of the answers to the issues I raise. I have tried to write this book in such a way that helps Christians in the South look at their lives and the church in a new way that will eventually lead to a genuine repentance and renewal among Christians in the South.

Whether you are offended at my perspective or completely resonate with it, my prayer is that the following pages will help you gain a more thorough understanding of the challenges and opportunities for Christians and churches in the South.

To that end, at the end of each chapter, I've included a set of passages for you to read, as well as a set of questions, to help you work through the text and the challenges discussed in the book.

While it's certainly helpful to work through these questions on your own, I also encourage you to discuss these passages and ideas in a small group so that you can get a deeper understanding of the challenges and hopefully come to a set of excellent solutions.

Questions for Reflection or Discussion

1. What are some of the things you love about where you live? How is that location distinct from other areas of the country?
2. In what ways has your local church been influential in your life?

Read Revelation 2:1-7 and reflect on the questions below.

1. How does your relationship with Christ now compare with what it was like when you first became a Christian? What are the key differences, and what are some of the reasons you can think of for those changes?
2. How has your church changed over the last few years? What are the key differences, and what are some of the reasons you can think of for those changes?
3. What good things did Jesus say characterized the church at Ephesus in his letter? Why is each of these traits important for a church to model?
4. When our relationship with God and others

becomes about duty, rather than love, what are some of the consequences?

5. If Jesus were to write a letter to your church, in what ways, if any, would He commend her? In what ways would he rebuke her?

6. What must your church remember, repent from, and act on if Jesus is not to remove your church's lampstand?

Read Revelation 3:14-21 and reflect on the questions below.

1. What does the "faithful and true witness" see when he looks at the Laodicean church (vv. 15-16)?

2. What appears to have made this church so distasteful to Christ that He had nothing good to say about it? What was the root of the Laodiceans' apathy?

3. How would you describe a church that is lukewarm? What are the dangers of this type of spiritual apathy for a church and individual Christians?

4. In what ways, if any, does your church family resemble the one in Laodicea?

Chapter 2

Southern Fried Feelings

"What people don't realize is how much religion costs. They think faith is a big electric blanket, when of course it is the cross."
- Flannery O' Connor

I don't consider myself an emotional person. I'm not callous or emotionally unavailable, but I don't cry at movies or anything. Not even funerals for that matter. At the same time, I'm human, which means I'm not above being impacted by my emotions, often in very powerful ways.

Looking back through my journal, it seems that the first noticeable physical symptoms came right after a short family vacation. My left eye twitched. I constantly pulled on my eyelid and rubbed the muscles surrounding it. Cold compresses, heating pads, "Icy Hot" (yes, near my eyes): Nothing worked. One of my parishioners, a physician, suggested I take a beta-blocker (whatever that is), but that seemed to me only a way to remedy the symptom, not deal with whatever was making my eye twitch. (Funny how that idea didn't come to me when I was putting "Icy Hot" around my eye).

Soon thereafter the twitching started in my left arm and left leg. On and off for many days, muscle groups large and small in those two limbs randomly and uncontrollably fired. A few days later, my left side went numb when I tried to sleep at night. By "left side," I mean face, torso, arm and leg.

In my humility (cough), I refused to go to the doctor, so I did what you would probably do in this situation: I asked Google about my symptoms. If you've never done this, let me warn you. Google wants you to have a horrible disease.

I searched Google hoping to find stretching exercises to correct a nerve out of whack or a set of best practices for reducing stress, but instead I diagnosed myself with Lou Gehrig's disease (ALS: Amyotrophic Lateral Sclerosis).

To be fair, one of the reasons I convinced myself I had ALS is because a year earlier, my mother was diagnosed with it. Her symptoms began differently, and it's quite rare for ALS to be shared from generation to generation, but common sense had no chance against my fear and Google's unquestionable wisdom. I had ALS.

So I went into crisis mode. I bought a life insurance policy that all but tempted my wife to have me murdered so she could be wealthier and have a new, healthy, sane husband. I organized all of our paperwork so that my death would not cause an undue burden on my soon-to-be rich family. I wrote tearful letters to friends and family to read after I died (now permanently disposed of). I planned one final family vacation, trying to time it so that I wouldn't be a physical burden on those I would travel with.

As it turns out, I didn't have ALS. I was clinically depressed, and that depression wreaked havoc not only on my body, but also on my ability to make choices and relate to others. During this time frame, I made countless decisions: some big, some small, some moral, some immoral, and some amoral. I shudder to think how my depression affected my mind and my relationships if it in any way compared to how it affected my body.

Faith and our Feelings

Even though the relationship between our minds, feelings, and behaviors is complex, we all have a personal preference when it comes to these things and how we make decisions. Of course, we try to be balanced, but our fallen nature and the fallen nature of those we are in relationship with makes it impossible for us to make choices in a perfectly balanced way. It's not that we ignore the other elements involved, but in the end, one of them trumps the others.

For example, I recently passed up an opportunity to attend my 20-year high school reunion. I had a decent list of reasonable excuses. We had a 6-week old baby that we weren't comfortable traveling with yet. Most of my genuine friends from high school were not attending. But the real reason I didn't attend is because I didn't want to relive high school. I suppose it's ironic I'm insecure about my high school insecurities, but that doesn't change the fact that seeing people from high school is as appealing to me as getting my teeth cleaned.

I made the decision in a similar way to how I make many other "left or right" (as opposed to "right or wrong") decisions on a daily basis: I ask a series of questions in an effort to make a wise decision, some of which relate to my feelings (or someone else's feelings) and some of which relate purely to facts. I try to be balanced in my approach, yet in the end, I usually go with what I *feel* is best. The facts are not the determining factor, neither is how my decision might affect others. Knowing the facts and the relational intricacies, I usually go with what feels right and live with the consequences.

This process is a common method of decision-making in the South. It's not that we southerners don't take in the facts, and it's not that we don't care about other people. For the most part, we just like to "feel" like we are choosing to do the right thing. And this process is not an unbiblical one. Scripture is full of stories highlighting the dominant role emotions play in decision-making, and often for good.

During the time that judges ruled the people of Israel, a woman named Naomi followed her husband Elimelech from their home in Judah to the land of Moab in search of relief from a famine. They had two sons (Mahlon and Chilion) who each married Moabite women (Orpah and Ruth). At some point Elimelech died, and not long thereafter, so did

Mahlon and Chilion, leaving Naomi with her Moabite daughters-in-law.

With no personal stake in Moab, and with improving agricultural conditions in Judah, Naomi set off for home, initially with her daughters-in-law in tow. But as they reached a certain point early in their journey, Naomi reasoned rather emotionally with her daughters-in-law for them to stay in Moab. Her simple and heartfelt blessing, though, was initially no match for Orpah and Ruth's desire to be with Naomi. They both pledged to travel with her to Judah and live with her.

Yet the wisdom and logic of an older woman became too much for one of the widows to bear. Tears flowing, Orpah turned around and headed home. Ruth, however, was not swayed. Once again, Naomi passionately reasoned with Ruth to stay, yet no amount of reason or logic could overcome Ruth's emotions associated with the potential loss of her relationship with Naomi. In a moving reply, Ruth pledged her devotion to Naomi.

This side of the gospel, we know that Ruth's devotion to Naomi was of the Lord. The entire arrangement worked out well for both of them, especially Ruth. She married an amazing guy and became part of both David and Jesus' ancestral line. None of these blessings would have happened had Ruth, like Orpah, listened to reason. Thankfully, she followed her heart.

Esther's situation was a little different. She was a Jew, but her ethnic and religious background was unknown to her pagan husband, the King of Assyria. One of the king's henchmen was using the king to wipe the Jewish people off the planet, and Esther alone was in a position to do something to save her people.

It was reasonable to conclude that Esther couldn't do anything about the plight of her people. If she approached the king in his inner courtyard without a personal invitation, she would likely die. If she died, her people would as well. Then again, it was also possible that Esther had been providentially placed in the king's palace for a special reason, perhaps to save her people.

With reason pulling her in both directions, Esther went with what felt right. She, along with all of her female servants and all the Jews in the capital, prayed and fasted for three days. Though it went against the law, Esther entered into the king's inner courtyard, where she was greeted warmly and given the opportunity to save her people.

While Ruth had every justifiable reason to not do what she did, Esther had reasons to go in either direction. Both of these women went with what felt best in full recognition of the facts, and it providentially paid off.

Faith in our Feelings

Feelings, though an important part of what it means to be human, are just as depraved as our minds, and therefore cannot be trusted. Simply because we feel something is true doesn't make it true. We must be wary of trusting our feelings to the degree that we use them as our de-facto filter for decision-making, even at the expense of biblical truth.

As a pastor, I spent a few weeks listening to one couple's struggles. Though I was not equipped to walk with them through their issues in a truly helpful way, I was able to identify certain patterns of behavior and reasoning that were hurting their marriage. Armed with this help, they transferred their counseling over to a professional, and my level of care went down several notches.

Weeks after our last session, one of them approached me with eyes full of tears. "The more I spend time with God, the more I feel like I'm supposed to get a divorce." To the best of my knowledge, nothing about this person's marriage justified divorce. The pain of working through their marital issues was so great, and the prospect of that pain going away through a divorce so promising, this person eventually justified the decision and believed God agreed.

We must resist the urge to believe we would never say or do something like that. The temptation to put our faith in our feelings is no respecter of persons. At one point or another, we have all put our faith in our feelings rather than in Jesus. We've chosen to gratify ourselves according to what feels good rather than be sanctified through an alignment of our feelings with the truth, and some of the Bible's most admirable people were just like us.

In 2 Samuel 11, David, the "man after God's own heart," trusted his emotions in ways that led to a lifetime of pain. Drawn by the allure of a peaceful spring day in his palace, David elected to stay in

Jerusalem rather than fight with his troops against the Ammonites. After an afternoon catnap, he went for a walk along the roof of his palace. From there, he saw a beautiful woman taking a ritualistic bath of purity. Her name was Bathsheba, the daughter of one of his best fighters, the granddaughter of one of his most trusted counselors, and the wife of one of his most honored soldiers.

Though the Law of God strictly prohibited adultery and called for the death penalty for anyone who committed it, "David sent messengers to get her, and when she came to him, he slept with her" (2 Samuel 11:4). Bathsheba became pregnant and shared the news with David, who then had her husband, Uriah, transferred home in hopes that he would sleep with Bathsheba and think he was the father of the child to come.

Uriah, however, had more integrity than David and refused to go to his home and sleep with his wife. David tried everything to convince Uriah to do it, even mocking his virility, but Uriah refused. Fearful of being found out, David sent Uriah to the front lines of the war where he was killed, and David married Bathsheba.

Adultery, deceit, murder and polygamy: all the result of David making choices with his feelings in spite of the truth. And if we, like David, are willing to forsake truth in order to act on our feelings, truth void of emotion has little hope of speaking correction into us. That is at least part of the reason the prophet Nathan used a story to confront David and call him to repentance. An emotionally charged behavior is best called out through an emotionally charging story, and Nathan dialed up a great one for a lowly shepherd boy turned wealthy king.

There were two men in a certain city, one rich and the other poor. The rich man had a large number of sheep and cattle, but the poor man had nothing except one small ewe lamb that he had bought. He raised it, and it grew up, living with him and his children. It shared his meager food and drank from his cup; it slept in his arms, and it was like a daughter to him. Now a traveler came to the rich man, but the rich man could not bring himself to take one of his own sheep or cattle to prepare for the traveler who had come to him. Instead, he took the poor man's lamb and prepared it for his guest (2 Samuel 12:2-4).

David, infuriated with the rich man in the story, called for him to die, but not before giving the poor man four lambs in place of the one he stole and killed. In the heat of that moment, Nathan passionately revealed the true intent of his story.

> *"You are the man! This is what the LORD God of Israel says: 'I anointed you king over Israel, and I delivered you from the hand of Saul. I gave your master's house to you and your master's wives into your arms, and I gave you the house of Israel and Judah, and if that was not enough, I would have given you even more. Why then have you despised the command of the LORD by doing what I consider evil? You struck down Uriah the Hittite with the sword and took his wife as your own wife—you murdered him with the Ammonite's sword (2 Samuel 12:7-9).*

David's response was as dramatic as it was simple: "I have sinned against the Lord" (2 Samuel 12:13). The Lord took David's sin away, but because David treated God with such contempt, the Lord took the life of the baby born to David by Bathsheba through a prolonged illness that led David to commune with God through prayer and fasting for a week.

Through David's experience, I am forced to fathom the degree to which my feelings influence my decision-making. I am challenged to consider all the ways my depression may have affected my choices as a husband, father, foster-parent, and pastor. I am pushed to ponder the things I might have unhealthy emotional attachments to. Most of all, I am called to give thanks for the grace and mercy of God who takes all of my emotionally-driven sin from me and redeems my mistake-ridden life for my good and His glory.

Faith with our Feelings

I was a racist through much of my childhood. Like other white people in the Mississippi Delta in the 1980s, I considered myself superior to just about anyone with black skin if only because my skin was white.

Slowly but surely, Jesus changed my heart on this matter, so much so that when our foster care license became active in May 2010, we were grateful to welcome two bi-racial little girls into our family (African-American and Hispanic).

Still, it was not a decision we made lightly. Though I knew our mostly white congregation would lovingly embrace the girls, only months earlier did someone anonymously place a note on the car of a visiting black family, informing them that "their kind" were not welcome. Pastoral ministry is demanding, and foster care is a time-intensive ministry that cannot be compromised. As one well-intentioned member asked, "Why did you take these children when you already have us to take care of?"

The decision-making process to become foster parents was one wrought with emotion, and life as a foster parent followed suit. At the peak of my frustration as a foster parent, I was an angry, bitter, mean dad, especially to the foster girls.

The oldest exhibited a lot of behaviors that would lead some therapists to diagnose her with Reactive Attachment Disorder. Without the same foundation of parenting as my other kids, my parenting skills and techniques were ineffective and even harmful. Rather than humbly accepting my weaknesses, I occasionally turned to anger to "straighten those kids out." I was an emotional disaster.

But God also used our foster care experience to accomplish things in and through the church. We saw our congregation warm up to the idea of missional living: Other families in the congregation followed God's lead to enter the foster care system, and at least two white couples in the congregation adopted black or bi-racial infants. These were great moments of joy and celebration for the church as a whole, for they gave us a taste of heaven and gave strong evidence to the gospel's power to a watching community.

If logic or reason had been our sole guide, we could have gone either direction with the decision to be foster parents. The same is true had feelings been our sole guide. Emotionally, I was ready to send the girls back into the system multiple times. Fortunately, reason saw me through my pain.

What I learned is that our feelings are not an "add-on" to our faith—something that we tack on to add value to our otherwise logical or reasonable choices. Nor are our feelings something that replace our faith altogether, for they are depraved and prone to lead us astray. Rather, our feelings are a significant part of our faith. They challenge us to believe things that we might otherwise see as unreasonable, and sanctify us as we are forced to act against them and in alignment with God's Word and the Holy Spirit. The answer is not "faith and feelings" or "faith in feelings," but "faith with feelings."

Questions for Reflection or Discussion

Read Ruth 1 and reflect on the questions below.

1. Given the social problems facing these widows, why do you think Naomi told Ruth and Orpah to return to their families?
2. How did Naomi bless her daughters-in-law? What did her words reveal about her relationship with Ruth and Orpah?
3. What can you surmise about Naomi, Ruth, and Orpah's character based on this emotional, parting conversation?
4. Though clearly emotional, both Ruth and Naomi confess God's sovereign control of events, each in her own way. What truth does each convey of God? Of themselves?
5. Have you ever experienced a time when you

were disappointed in God because the circumstances you faced were not what you expected? How was your faith tested?

Chapter 3

Keeping the Peace

"The operation of the Church is entirely set up for the sinner; which creates much misunderstanding among the smug."
- Flannery O'Connor

I've fought a lot of battles in my last 15 years of ministry, and I've learned a lot of lessons as a result. For example:

- Some parents of teenagers are not OK with the use of clips from "The Simpson's."
- The only way for someone to get saved is if they are given the opportunity to walk down the aisle and ask me about it right after I preach.
- $6,000 annually for donuts is a wise investment in student ministry.
- Let kids choose their own roommates for camps and retreats.

- If you like your Bible study curriculum, you can keep it: period.
- The KJV was authorized by Jesus, not James.

So when I got more than a few complaints about our worship pastor leading from the stage with his shirt untucked, I was reluctant to bring it up with him. It didn't really bother me all that much, for very little about the church was traditional or formal in nature. The church office was in a doublewide portable building that shook violently in moderate thunderstorms.

We gathered in a barebones multipurpose building that, like most "cafegymatoriums," failed to support any purpose very well. Worship music was contemporary in style, and it wasn't uncommon for our worship pastor to lead from behind the drum set. Taking all these things and more into consideration, the untucked shirt actually fit in better than the alternatives.

Contrary to my presumption, our worship leader wasn't rebelling against tradition, but concealing a gun: a Glock model 22 .40 caliber in an "inside the waistband" concealment holster. So to keep the peace with our critics, he settled on a Ruger

LCR .38 caliber special in an ankle holster. I was surprised to learn that he carried a concealed weapon, but I was shocked to learn that many more members carried as well. An employee of a local shooting range once commented that our congregation was the most secure in the area because so many members carried guns.

With all the "peace makers" tucked away on any given Sunday, one might expect congregational life to have been free of conflict all together. But while carrying a piece may help keep the peace, a church needs something else entirely to make peace.

Engaging in Conflict

Like most young boys, I experienced my share of fights growing up. Like fewer young boys, I started most of them, and lost even more. This was primarily due to the fact that my mouth was larger than my biceps.

The relationship between those two body parts was cyclical: I routinely used words and wit to combat physical bullying that I could not match with brawn, and I brought fights upon myself by speaking harshly to others. Of course, there were times when others set out to harm me simply because they knew they could easily take me. I had the physical frame of a Charms Blow-Pop: a pencil-thin frame with a large head, so everyone was confident they could lick me. Be it a brawny bully's insecurities, my over-confident tongue, or some combination of the two, my childhood was ripe with conflict.

I had higher expectations for relationships in the church, though. This is ironic given that expectation is really nothing more than premeditated resentment. And that resentment is a form of conflict. But it's the truth. All hell could break loose at home or school, but on Wednesday nights and Sunday mornings, conflict was not a possibility. The church, as I understood it, was where all the good people were, and good people don't fight or argue about things that don't really matter, and they certainly don't pick fights with one another.

I'm sure that some churches would love for that to be their reputation, but if that were the case, it's the last church I would visit. A church void of conflict is a church void of the gospel. For years, I foolishly believed that a gathering of Jesus followers was a group of good people who had it all together and never fought with one another, when the clear biblical teaching about the church is that it's a gathering of people confessing their need for Jesus, which presumes their lives are conflicted and broken. In fact, the only thing Christians have in common is their confession that they are broken and in need of rescue by the One who was broken and resurrected. It's not a gathering of people who are more like Jesus as much as it is a gathering of people who know they need Jesus.

What is needed among Christians and the church in the South is not necessarily less conflict, but a gospel-centered methodology for handling it and working through it. We need to recognize that conflict among Christians in the church is ultimately a spiritual thing, and is therefore an inevitable and necessary part of living the Christian life. There are biblical ways to handle it, and none of them are particularly southern.

Southern Fried Resolutions

William was a youth pastor in a moderate-sized Baptist church in Arkansas. When he entered into his seventh year of service at the church, William felt like he was just beginning to reap the fruit of his ministry. However, the new families entering into the youth ministry with them a desire for their kids to be busier with church events and for the weekly programs to be more entertaining.

William never heard about these opinions personally. Parents of the students spoke among themselves, to the personnel committee, and even to the pastor. The pastor, rather than directing these parents to speak with William directly about their concerns, agreed to speak with William for them.

William listened to the pastor and took his concerns seriously, attempting to implement changes that didn't seriously conflict with his philosophy of ministry that had guided him faithfully for years. He held parent meetings, spoke openly and honestly, but was never directly approached by the parents who, despite his best efforts, were still not satisfied. Discouraged, William sent his resume to various opportunities as he saw fit, convinced that those new parents would never speak directly to him, much less hear him out about his convictions in ministry.

Leave it to a bunch of southern church people to ruin a perfect opportunity to see the gospel work in the life of a student pastor, students and their parents. It is so much more southern to keep the peace than have God turn us into people who make peace, and we have many tactics at our disposal.

Some of us bully others when conflict arises. At the expense of a relationship with someone we disagree with, we use our intellect, our ability to argue, or the power associated with our position to force people into seeing things our way. Others of us go on the defensive. In the midst of conflict, we might move to justify or defend ourselves, minimizing our exposure to our own shortcomings.

Still others dodge the conflict entirely. We may divert the conversation to a different topic or attack the credibility of the person bringing the charge, but we most certainly don't see conflict as an opportunity for peacemaking. Finally, some of us act passively. We might be very emotional about the situation, but we won't show any signs or say any words about it to those directly involved. In these moments, we conclude that all conflict is wrong and should be endured quietly in the name of "love." We become more interested in keeping people from being hurt than about being reconciled to God's truth. We tell ourselves that we are holding it in because we want to protect others, but really it's all about us and what we want.

Regardless of our tactics, the result is the same: lies and shame instead of truth and reconciliation. The southern church must learn to see conflict between Christians as a prime opportunity for the gospel to shine and have an impact on both believer and unbeliever, rather than something to cover in shame like it never happened. It all starts with an understanding of the nature of conflict.

The Gift of Conflict

Conflict among Christians is a spiritual issue. It involves the work of a supernatural being named Satan. Paul writes in Ephesians 6:11-12, "Put on the full armor of God so that you can stand against the tactics of the Devil. For our battle is not against flesh and blood, but against the rulers, against the authorities, against the world powers of this darkness, against the spiritual forces of evil in the heavens."

Ultimately, conflict among Christians is rooted in a cosmic battle between supernatural powers that impacts us directly and indirectly. Only through putting on the spiritual armor and prayer do we win such conflicts (Ephesians 6:13-18).

But we can't point fingers at Satan as the only source of spiritual conflict in our churches. Consider James 4:1-4:

What is the source of wars and fights among you? Don't they come from the cravings that are at war within you? You desire and do not have. You murder and covet and cannot obtain. You fight and war. You do not have because you do not ask. You ask and don't receive because you ask with wrong motives, so that you may spend it on your evil desires. Adulteresses! Don't you know that friendship with the world is hostility toward God?

In the same way that Adam and Eve could not blame their conflict with God and each other on Satan, neither can we. James states that we are spiritually and morally dysfunctional, and this is a major cause for conflicts among Christians.

Because conflict is spiritual, it's also inevitable. "For the desires of the flesh are against the Spirit, and the desires of the Spirit are against the flesh, for these are opposed to each other, to keep you from doing the things you want to do" (Galatians 5:17). In other words, while we can be disheartened or disappointed when conflict arises in a church, we should, by no means, be caught off guard. We are relational and spiritual beings with conflict raging inside of us between our flesh and the Spirit, and that conflict spills out into our relationships.

Thankfully, God has a purpose for conflict. You might even say that we need it. Near the end of Luke's gospel, Jesus and Peter had a conversation about the conflict Peter would undergo as a result of Jesus' arrest and crucifixion.

Jesus told Peter, "Simon, Simon, look out! Satan has asked to sift you like wheat. But I have prayed for you that your faith may not fail. And you, when you have turned back, strengthen your brothers" (Luke 22:31-32a).

Jesus taught Peter that the "sifting" he would undergo would put him into the position to strengthen his brothers later. The conflict was the necessary means by which God accomplished His redemptive purposes for Peter, the disciples, and eventually the church.

When we recognize the true nature of conflict in the church, we begin to see it as the gift it really is. Conflict is an opportunity for Christians in the church to remember and believe the gospel. And when we confess the gospel with one another, we make peace with one another, which is an entirely different thing than keeping peace.

Keeping peace may be easier, but making peace is biblical. This clarifies why Jesus said, "The peacemakers are blessed, for they will be called sons of God" (Matthew 5:9). The people who confess the gospel to themselves are people who welcome God to make peace in their conflict because they believe that God made peace with their ultimate conflict with sin.

Letters to the Pastor

I don't have a file cabinet in my office at the moment, so inside of a cardboard file box in my home is a file labeled "notes of encouragement." There are about 50 or so cards and letters that I received over the last twenty years of church ministry. Every now and then, I would pull those notes out and read them again in order to be encouraged or inspired during difficult times.

I don't have a folder for all the notes and letters I received from people expressing anger, frustration, or bitterness. I eventually trashed those. If they were sent anonymously, I didn't read them at all. If they were signed, and if church members wrote them, I tried my level best to deal with the issues in a biblical fashion. Because sinners and unbelievers were involved, results varied. Some conflicts were resolved beautifully in a way that truly glorified Jesus. Others, like the very first conflict I dealt with, ended sadly.

Less than two months into a pastorate, I received a relatively long, typewritten letter from a member that detailed all of the reasons three of the other ministers on staff should have been fired. The allegations were not broad or generic, but specific and detailed. With the letter in hand, I met individually with each staff member and went through his or her version of events. Each of them agreed to meet with the accuser, so I took my notes and the letter back in to my office and called the church member.

The conversation that ensued was not a pleasant one. This person had no interest in resolving the issues, nor did they desire to live in biblical community with church leaders. The purpose in writing was to equip me with the "truth" so that I could do their bidding. This individual was aggressive in writing the letter to me, defensive when confronted, evasive with every attempt I made to reconcile, and pretended like nothing happened for a few weeks before leaving the church. Sometimes it's easier to believe that we are better than other people than it is to believe the gospel.

Troublemaking Peacemakers

Anybody who attempts to write a book is comfortable in the arena of ideas, but because I've served as a pastor in a local church for most of my working years, I appreciate the value of practical application. So if the idea of "believing the gospel more" is too nebulous to aid you in your quest to make peace, consider Jesus' very practical instruction in Matthew 18:15-17.

"If your brother sins against you, go and rebuke him in private. If he listens to you, you have won your brother. But if he won't listen, take one

or two more with you, so that by the testimony of two or three witnesses every fact may be established. If he pays no attention to them, tell the church. But if he doesn't pay attention even to the church, let him be like an unbeliever and a tax collector to you.

The major difference between doing what Jesus teaches and doing what we southerners think is polite is that Jesus' method gives all parties involved multiple opportunities to think about the gospel. Our southern fried methods only serve our self-interests.

The person who wrote the letter to me could have had multiple rewarding personal conversations with each staff member. If those did not bring a resolution, I could have gotten involved to help bring about a solution. If that didn't work, some of sort of church leadership body or even the entire congregation could have had the opportunity to see the gospel at work. The entire event may have ended the same way (with this person leaving the church), but at least the gospel would have been preached to all many times over, rather than Satan's methods of passive-aggressive behavior.

We can follow Jesus' teaching even if we don't necessarily see how the gospel applies at that moment. When we choose to obey even when we don't appreciate or understand why, God uses those moments to form us into people who see their daily need for Him more and more. The more we obey according to the gospel, the more we believe the gospel. The more we believe the gospel, the more we obey. Our obedience to the gospel helps us believe it, and our believing leads us to obey.

This process is the essence of what it means to be Christian: becoming ever more aware of our sin and ineptitude and ever more grateful for Jesus' perfect obedience and sacrifice. We don't think more of ourselves as we become more like Christ, but less. And people who think less of themselves aren't afraid to make trouble to make peace.

Questions for Reflection or Discussion

Read Matthew 5:3-12 and reflect on the questions below.

1. How do the Beatitudes in verses 3-6 relate to the promises that follow them?

2. What kind of mourning do you feel Jesus is talking about in verse 4?

3. When you think of someone who is a good example of meekness (v. 5), what is that person like? What do you admire about them?

4. What do the four attitudes in verses 7-12 (merciful, pure in heart, peacemaker, and righteousness) have in common?

5. How do the Beatitudes in these verses relate to the promises that follow them?

6. According to v. 9, what evidence shows that you are a peacemaker?

7. When might pursuing God's peace cause trouble in our world? Why is this the case?

Read Mathew 18:15-17 and reflect on the questions below.

1. How does Scripture instruct us to approach the one who sins against us? In contrast to speaking publicly, what benefit does a private confrontation offer for both parties?

2. How many conflict situations do we discuss openly with someone not in the conflict

before ever speaking to the offending spouse, friend, or fellow believer? What does this say about our motives and beliefs?

3. What qualities would you need to look for when choosing these one or two witnesses?

4. Why is this process so important? Which step do you struggle with the most?

5. Who are you currently in conflict with? Will you choose to believe the gospel and act in accordance with Jesus' teaching in this passage? Will you choose to act even though you may not agree and let Him help your unbelief?

6. Does your church have an intentional means by which it can follow Jesus' teaching as an organization?

7. What does unresolved conflict among Christians say to a lost world?

Chapter 4

Bless Your Heart

"Please help me dear God to be a good writer... don't let me ever think... that I was anything but the instrument for your story."
- Flannery O'Connor

I couldn't find a ministerial position immediately after graduating divinity school, so my wife and I moved to Dallas, TX where friends and jobs were plentiful. We invested the bulk of our savings into a dated, two-bedroom condominium near the expressway north of downtown.

The condo was more than adequate for our needs, but my wife and I are the kind of people who see great potential in everything and everybody, and this place was no exception. "What an accomplishment it would be," we said, "to renovate this place on our own and flip it for a profit." It mattered not that I had flunked out of the School for the Mechanically Declined. We were going to climb the property ladder, and no one would stop us. Like any good southerner, I was a proud do-it-yourselfer.

I began the extensive project with my father-in-law. I did not know him well at the time, but I did know that he was quite the handyman. On the first day, we prepped all the rooms for painting and then started painting one of the bedrooms. I had clearly underestimated the amount of work to be done and overestimated my abilities to do it well. At the end of our first day, I complained to my father-in-law about our lack of progress. He kindly patted me on the back and said, "Bless your heart." What else was there to say?

Nevertheless, we persevered. With the painting done and my father-in-law gone, my wife and I turned our attention to the master bathroom. First, I used a belt sander to smooth out the adobe-style mud that had been plastered on the walls. Dust filled our home for weeks. We washed our sheets daily. It wasn't a case of severe dandruff or leprosy. We just had tons of dried mud dust in our home.

Next came the bathroom floor. We pulled up the blue carpet and then the toilet (perhaps the most disgusting thing you will ever do in your life) and prepped the floor for new ceramic tile.

I used a special chemical instead of water to mix the mud, one that allowed me to secure the tile to the floor quicker so that I could conceivably tile and grout the floor on the same day. I didn't have enough money or self-confidence to use a wet saw for cutting the tile, so I rented a scorer. For those of you who have not cut tile in this way, imagine trying to carve a tomato with a rolling pin.

Despite my inadequacies and insufficiencies, the bathroom turned out fine, which gave us the confidence to put tile down in the other bathroom and in the kitchen. Seven months later, we had a fully remodeled home that God would call us to leave a few weeks later. We were incredibly proud of our accomplishment. Even though we lost a little money in the end, the experience helped us with future renovations, most of which have been fruitful.

The Dark Side of Pride

We southerners are proud of our pride. A sense of pride in one's work is a wonderful virtue. When we take pride in our accomplishments, we build a positive reputation for ourselves and establish trust with others. Think about it. When was the last time you chose to eat at restaurant whose cleaning service or chef strived for mediocrity, or bought gas from the station whose facilities showed the greatest amount of neglect? Our nearly subconscious choice is to relate to and do business with those who are proud of themselves and their efforts. We trust them because they clearly care about themselves and their work.

The problem with this virtue is that it easily collapses on itself in the economy of the gospel. At no point can we take pride in our efforts and expect them to be an adequate basis for God to accept us. To illustrate this point, Jesus told a parable in Luke 18:9-14 about a man who took great pride in His spiritual accomplishments, and even gave thanks to God for them.

His public prayer was this: "God, I thank You that I'm not like other people—greedy, unrighteous, adulterers, or even like this tax collector. I fast twice a week; I give a tenth of everything I get (Luke 18:11b-12)." I'm initially drawn to this man. If he was as holy, content, faithful, generous, and prayerful as he implied, then he was the kind of religious leader I want to follow. I want to follow a person who takes pride in spiritual accomplishments and is thankful to God for them.

I do not want to follow the other guy in this parable, referred to by Jesus and the religious leader as a tax collector. "But the tax collector, standing far off, would not even raise his eyes to heaven but kept striking his chest and saying, 'God, turn your wrath from me—a sinner!'" Who desires to follow the example of a social outcast who publicly confesses his sin? Not me. My natural desire is to follow the person with the long list of accomplishments.

Jesus, however, taught us not to follow the one who has pride in his spiritual accomplishments, but the one who acknowledges such accomplishments can never adequately serve as a basis for God's acceptance. "I tell you, (the tax collector) went down to his house justified rather than the other; because everyone who exalts himself will be humbled, but the one who humbles himself will be exalted (v. 14)."

Jesus' teaching flies in the face of a southern culture vehemently committed to hard work and pride in one's efforts. In the economy of the American South, it is enough to work hard and be grateful to a good God for making us that way. Yet such thinking is contrary to the gospel of grace. When we believe that others accept us on the basis of great work, we conclude that God does as well. Nothing could be further from the truth, and few things hurt worse than learning this lesson.

Christmas Drama

If there was ever a ministry for a church to be proud of, the Christmas production at one church I served fit the bill. What began in 1980's as a simple "walk through Bethlehem" in which a few hundred people strolled through and experienced a realistic reenactment of the birth of Jesus, steadily ballooned into a two-hour production about the life of Jesus.

Eventually, the church built a warehouse-style building designed exclusively for the purpose of the production that sat 2,700. In 2008, 40,066 people attended 18 performances, 432 of whom "rededicated" their life to Jesus, and 69 of whom made "first time decisions." It was not uncommon for the church to report hundreds of "first time decisions" in the 1990's and 2000's. Prior to my arrival in 2008, the event tied with the city zoo's Christmas light display for the best Christmas event in the area. In 2012, the American Bus Association ranked the production in its top 100 events in North America. Every year, thousands of dollars and hundreds of comments came in to the church unsolicited, many of them like this one from a gentleman who lived about 70 miles away.

I must admit, I was overwhelmed and filled with joy. I could hardly sleep that night and I've just been praising Him. I've told my co-workers about it and I have encouraged them to attend with their family. I believe in what you are doing and I know God is pleased. This drama looks like something I would see on TBN – Praise the Lord. My life is forever changed. Thank you for rekindling the spirit back in me.

While the quality of the production was quite good for the level of financial investment and expertise of the lay people leading it, not everyone found it edifying. One pastor I invited had this biting, sarcastic reaction: "Keith Green, 1971, Jesus Christ Superstar, Bill Gaither, and Larry Norman all called and they want their musical back." He could have said that the production was uniquely southern and profoundly dated, but that wouldn't have been as humorous (or hurtful, depending on your perspective).

Love it or leave it, no one can deny the production was the pride and joy of many in the congregation. Such pride was taken in it by some that any attempt to adjust it, other than adding more performances, was deemed a threat to it. In the same way that the Pharisee in Luke 18 did not know faith apart from his accomplishments, some in the church did not know faith apart from the production. Yet the congregation was not alone in its struggle with pride in its accomplishments.

A Personal Confession

For the first two years of the pastorate, I generally humbled myself before God and begged Him frequently to do a work in the church. I was a clumsy, clueless first-time pastor who felt queasy just making hospital visits, so prayer came easily. And God was faithful. He answered my prayers in profound ways, though not in ways that did not cause some in the church to become frustrated.

Nevertheless, God was working, developing a spirit of humility in church leaders and members alike.

After two years, things settled down significantly. Most of the objective and subjective "church health" markers pointed in a positive direction. I entered in to a two-week vacation overseas utterly exhausted but giving thanks to God for His provision. In fact, things were so much better that upon my return, I subtly, if not unconsciously, began to take pride in my pastoral accomplishments. As I did so, things began to unravel.

The worse things got over the next 18 months, the more prideful I became and the harder I tried to combat issues in my own wisdom and strength. In turn, I became increasingly depressed. God really does oppose the proud and give grace to the humble (James 4:6).

Rather than immediately repent of my pride, I turned it toward my depression. I read some amazing, Gospel-centered books on depression. I became engrossed with wellness (chiropractic care, diet, exercise, etc.) as a means of coping. I took more time to be with family during the day. I gave more of myself to the aspects of pastoral ministry that gave me joy. I took little 2-day vacations with my family and went on more date nights. While all of these things are wonderful and helpful for depression, they could not compensate for the pride that was driving it.

Only in retrospect did I see the irony. I was pastoring a church through its own pride in its accomplishments while dealing with my own at the same time. The end result was the same for both. The production ended and so did my pastorate. Both church and pastor learned that we couldn't become more proud of our accomplishments than Jesus' accomplishment, not even if we gave Him thanks for those accomplishments.

Bless Your Heart

While the effects of pride are devastating on an individual or a congregation, they are also detrimental to our ministry to others. Remember the Pharisee's prayer in Luke 18? He ticked off his enviable list of spiritual accomplishments with a judgmental spirit specifically aimed the tax collector. If the Pharisee had been a southerner, he would have said, "Lord, I thank you that I am not like that tax collector, bless his heart."

"Bless your heart" is a phrase us southerners use as a way of politely masking our sense of moral superiority. For example, when someone is telling a story that we could not care less about, our response will be, "Bless your heart," meaning, "I'm sorry your life is so meaningless and that I've been caught up in it." When someone is dressed distastefully for a given occasion and we say, "Bless her heart," what we mean is, "How could she not know that those pants make her bottom look like challah bread?"

A "bless your heart" mindset may be polite and southern, but it is also very sinful. A message of grace and love mixed with an attitude of moral superiority is either rejected out of hand as the smugness it is or eagerly embraced by those who believe they, too, have much to be proud of. Either way, the end result is a church full of people who believe they are superior to the very community they are called to serve.

Jesus' Accomplishment

What is the solution to such a dilemma? How do we avoid becoming legalistic, holier-than-thou, "bless your heart," passive-aggressive jerks, yet still work hard and represent Jesus well? Jesus answered this question very clearly in Luke 18:14: "Whoever humbles himself will be exalted."

Humility is not thinking less of ourselves, nor is it thinking of ourselves less. Humility is choosing a posture of submission to one who is truly worthy. It presumes the existence of someone greater than us. If we are going to obey Jesus' command to humble ourselves, then we can only do so by acknowledging and living according to Him who is truly great.

What did Jesus do that makes Him great and worthy of our humble submission? He humbled Himself! Paul explains it beautifully in Philippians 2:5-11.

(Jesus) emptied Himself by assuming the form of a slave, taking on the likeness of men. And when He had come as a man in His external form, He humbled Himself by becoming obedient to the point of death — even to death on a cross. For this reason God highly exalted Him and gave Him the name that is above every name, so that at the name of Jesus every knee will bow — of those who are in heaven and on earth and under the earth — and every tongue should confess that

Jesus Christ is Lord to the glory of God the Father.

Because God humbled Himself, died and rose again in His greatness, then God's people must humble themselves to His authority and tout His greatness, not their own. This true humility does not lead to mediocrity or indifference when it comes to service or work, but to a level of excellence that leads others to Him who is most excellent. As Paul writes in 2 Corinthians 10:17-18, "So, 'the one who boasts must boast in the Lord.' For it is not the one commending himself who is approved, but the one the Lord commends."

Whereas the Pharisee in Luke 18 gave thanks to God for his good works and relied upon them for his identity before God and man, Christians understand good works to be a window through which others see Jesus' saving work. Hence, they do not boast in their accomplishments, but in their weaknesses and Jesus' greatness. The way that we make great accomplishments for the Kingdom of God is by continually pointing to the greatness of Jesus demonstrated in His life, death, and resurrection.

Our calling is to constantly espouse His great accomplishment, not any of our own, for apart from

His accomplishment our works have no meaning or value. Christians and their churches are exalted to the degree that they boast in the grace of God, and they are humbled to the degree that they take pride in their own efforts. God will get the glory He deserves. The only question is how long it will take us to give it to Him.

Questions for Reflection and Discussion

Read Luke 18:9-14 and consider the following questions.

1. Compare and contrast the Pharisee and the tax collector. What character traits are revealed in their respective prayers? In what ways are the Pharisee and the tax collector similar? In what ways are they different?

2. If you were one of the people listening to Jesus that day, what impact do you think the parable would have had on you? How would your thinking about God and righteousness have changed?

3. Like the Pharisee, are you thankful to God for the good things you do? Are you trusting in

those good things to make you right before God?

4. Is there a ministry by your church that the congregation takes great pride in yet also trusts in to validate its existence?

Read Philippians 2:1-11 and consider the following questions.

1. Why might dwelling on the person of Jesus Christ lead to the kind of humility called for in this passage?

2. What would it mean for you to have the mind of Christ? Why do you think Paul called for the mind of Christ instead of the actions of Christ?

3. Though culture often views humility as a weakness, in what ways did Jesus' humility convey and require strength?

4. Why do you think the church might have sung words like these in their early days? How would singing these words serve as both a protection for the church and as a motivation to the church?

Chapter 5

Know Your Motives

"I am very handy with my advice, and then when anybody appears to be following it, I get frantic."
- Flannery O' Connor.

There is much to love about pastoral ministry in the South. The joy of preaching and teaching the Bible is unparalleled. Experiencing the Word of God come alive in people through conversation and prayer over an excellent cup of coffee (or sweet tea) is electrifying. Facilitating a discussion with a leadership team about the mission of the church is exhilarating. To pray about and explore the ways a church should fulfill its mission is a stimulating enterprise. But the one thing I consistently loathe about pastoral ministry is making announcements. Few southern church traditions are as polarizing as the Sunday morning announcement.

Role-playing as the Minister of Announcements is tricky business. On one hand, I know that most people don't read a bulletin or newsletter, and

I desire to honor the hard work and servant hearts of the lay leaders and staff who rightfully desire their event or ministry opportunity to be successful. On the other hand, I know that if I launch into a list of events as if all of them are highly important, I give the impression that everything is always crucial to the life of the church. Most people inherently know that isn't the case, so they tend to turn a deaf ear as announcements are made.

I've served in or attended a number of churches and have witnessed many attempts to alleviate this problem. Some churches take a video recording of someone presenting the various events and service opportunities and play that video in the service. This method relieves the Minister of Announcements of wondering where he stands with that person who likes to drop a last-minute announcement bomb on him as he walks on stage, and also spares him from the feeling that he's over-communicating to the point that he's not communicating at all.

Other churches don't even bother with making announcements. The assumption is that members read the bulletin, newsletter, mail, email, blog, etc. and are willingly informed. But most churches I've served or attended generally leave it up the Minister of Announcements to convince the congregation that participating in a specific event or ministry opportunity is worth their while.

The burden of motivating volunteers to do anything is a substantial one. Church leaders cannot force compliance, nor can they threaten to remove any perceived "benefits" of church life should members choose not to serve or attend. Nevertheless, we church leaders have our ways, and the best (and worst) of these are southern to the core: we seek to personally gratify members or guilt their conscience into obedience.

Potlucks and Personal Gratification

Having pastored for many years, I've become an expert at virtually everything related to a potluck meal. I know that older men tend to carry their napkins and plastic utensils in their shirt pockets, keeping both hands free for carrying plates and drinks. I know that country gravy covers a multitude of cooking sins. I know that macaroni and cheese is a vegetable. I know that if I don't tell the church to bring an entrée or a salad, they will all almost certainly bring a dessert. I know that vegans never attend, and diabetics can no longer participate. I know it's unkind to wince at even the most horrible-tasting dish, and I've learned how to spread out a bad serving on my plate to make it look like I ate a lot of it.

I know to pay attention to who brings what as best I can, and to try just about everything that I can, if only to make insecure old ladies feel better about themselves. I know that the odds of an intestinal illness are elevated, and that cleanliness is only possible in heaven.

I know that timing is everything. If I am in line early, I'll be talked about as a selfish, impatient glutton, and if I go too late, I won't be able to say I tried Ms. So-and-So's green bean casserole. I know that no matter what, I have to eat something. A pastor who doesn't eat something at a potluck is perceived as a snob in the South.

This is ironic because I partially credit years of potlucks for turning me into something of a foodie: one who has a heightened or refined sense of interest in food and beverages. Though my rate of metabolism is slowing as I near the age of 40, I am still capable of putting down an inordinate amount of food. But because of my age, I've grown out of the "anything will do" frame of mind and have pretty high standards when it comes to food quality. I'm not (yet) a snob about it (I can't think of a pizza I wouldn't eat), but I'm convinced that food is one of the few areas of life where it's healthy for me to ask, "What's in it for me?" In some way, I'm always asking, "How is this food personally gratifying?" be it through the lens of convenience, cost, quality or number of calories.

The filter of personal gratification may be the primary way we decide if anything is worth participating in, even something of eternal importance. Think about the ways we react to the simplest of changes at the church, and you quickly realize that much of our willingness to support or be a part of something is built around our personal desires. Change the Sunday school classrooms? But that's been *my* classroom for years! Change the worship schedule to make room for a growing congregation? How will I beat the Methodists to lunch?

Asking "What's in it for me?" can be a healthy form of motivation sometimes. One of the reasons Christians gather on Sundays is for the mutual edification of believers—to meet one another's needs and enjoy one another's company. Troubles arise, however, when we conclude that God and His church are *about* us, not simply *for* us.

Perhaps the first people to learn this lesson were Ananias and Sapphira. In the church's early moments, things went incredibly well. God's grace was abundant in the church, and the gospel was preached consistently with great power. Members were strongly united, so much so that they didn't look at any of their material possessions as their own.

No one in the church had any real material needs "because all those who owned lands or houses sold them, brought the proceeds of the things that were sold, and laid them at the apostles' feet. This was then distributed for each person's basic needs" (Acts 4:34-35). The church was *for* its members, but it wasn't *about* its members.

In that moment, Ananias and Sapphira made the church's mission about themselves. Like others, they sold a piece of property and donated a *portion* of the proceeds to the church. This apparently selfless act was actually quite selfish, for they told the church that they gave *all* of the proceeds. They wanted the benefit of looking like generous church members with the added benefit of having a little extra cash on hand. The donation wasn't about the church or its mission, but about them.

Peter, by the power of the Holy Spirit, knew of their motives and their lie. He called them out, and the judgment God immediately brought on them both was severe: death. The message was clear. God designed the church to be *for* His people, but not *about* His people. "What's in it for me?" cannot be the primary way we decide how to participate in the life and mission of the church.

Guilty Conscience

If there's anything good about a selfishly motivated church member, it's that they are at least motivated. Frequently, church leaders have the opposite problem: members who cannot or will not serve or participate for any variety of reasons.

In response, church leaders commonly resort to bludgeoning members with guilt so that they will eventually choose to be a part of whatever program or ministry planned. Maybe you've heard or even used statements like the following at church.

- You'd better share your faith because if you don't, the blood of those people will be on your hands.
- We've prayed about it, and we are convinced that no matter how you feel, it is God's will for you to teach the three year-old class this year.
- If just one person comes to know Christ because of your commitment to this ministry, it will be worth it.

The kind of guilt exhibited in statements like these is what Paul calls "worldly grief" (2 Corinthians 7:10). Over time, this kind of motivation does incredible harm to the relationship between leaders and followers, and thus great harm to the church as a whole. At first, people may do what leaders want them to do, but they only do it to alleviate their guilt. As these guilt-driven experiences add up, so does resentment. It may take years, but people eventually realize that complying only gives them temporary relief from their guilt, so they willingly choose to endure the anger of those heaping guilt on them, which only leads them to resent their leaders more.

It's a vicious cycle that can only end in severed relationships and a fractured church.

Because I'm a foodie, I've got a fancy coffee maker. I don't roast or even grind my own beans, but I do take great care in making a great pot of coffee, of which a brewer plays a significant role. As it so happens, I live in an area where the tap water has a high mineral content. After a year of pouring hard water into my highfalutin coffee maker, the brass valve between the stainless steel water tank and brew basket clogged.

This is how guilt works as a motivator: for a time, it can boost giving or increase attendance at rehearsals, but eventually it creates bitterness in the heart of church people. They soon stop participating, and the church quickly stops functioning.

Gospel Motivation

Motivation is a complicated social science. There are a myriad of theories as to what kinds of motivation are proper in various situations. We humans are as fickle as we are predictable, so one can never be quite sure what kind of motivation is appropriate and successful for a given situation.

That's not to say, however, that there are no appropriate or helpful motivational principles in the Bible for leaders and participants alike.

Early in Paul's missionary, church-planting life, the church in Judea needed money. Paul had the responsibility of collecting it from various congregations he either started or visited, and the church in Corinth was one of those churches. Ironically, Paul did not have the best relationship with the church in Corinth, so asking them to give generously to another church was a sensitive matter. It was a big "ask" of people he was quite good at upsetting.

It's that backstory that makes Paul's motivational appeal in 2 Corinthians 8 and 9 all the more beautiful. First, Paul testified to the grace of God working in the lives of others. Multiple churches in the nearby region of Macedonia, though they were in a severe state of persecution and economic affliction, gave joyfully and well beyond their means. Then Paul pointed out that the Corinthians, by God's grace, had those same characteristics when it came to things like faith, preaching, and hard work. Therefore, said Paul, they should apply those same gifts to their giving.

At the end of his appeal, Paul pointed to the gospel. Jesus' gift of salvation was immeasurably abundant and utterly undeserved, and that gift should inform their giving. Interestingly, Paul never attempted to guilt the Corinthians into giving, but he did let them know that their generosity might one day benefit them. At that moment, the Judean church was in need. But one day, the Corinthians might need the Judeans. Therefore, they should give (2 Corinthians 8:1-15). By communicating the gospel, Paul sought to motivate and inspire the Corinthians to give.

Similarly, Peter encouraged church leaders to live the gospel so as to inspire their members. In 1 Peter 5, Peter mentioned sins to which church leaders are prone, as well as the antidotes to those sins. First, some leaders are lazy. They must be compelled to serve. Whether they are lazy by choosing to do nothing and creating a set of circumstances to justify their laziness, or lazy by allowing others to dictate their agenda, all that matters is that laziness is something to which church leaders are prone and must avoid.

Other times, leaders are selfish. They can accept the authority of ministry but shirk the corresponding responsibility. And we are all too familiar with the cases of church leaders who enter ministry for personal benefit, be it financially or out of a desire to have power over people's lives (1 Peter 5:1-3).

Peter's overarching antidote to these sins is for leaders to choose freely and willingly to serve, so that church members will follow their example. Interestingly, he unashamedly tells these elders that by doing so, they get something pretty amazing in return: "And when the chief Shepherd appears, you will receive the unfading crown of glory" (1 Peter 5:4). By pondering the truths of the gospel and the riches of heaven, leaders are inspired to serve in such a way that motivates their followers to live for the glory of heaven.

Both Paul and Peter turned to Jesus and the gospel to inspire and motivate others. The gospel is precisely what church leaders and members alike should look to when it comes to a proper motivation for serving. Even something as mundane as giving or listening to announcements on Sunday mornings can be a powerful opportunity to preach or hear the gospel.

If you're a pastor loathing the task of talking about yet another potluck, see if you can't find a fun and creative way to talk about Jesus as you talk about who brings an entrée or a dessert. Everything you have to say will be more meaningful to you and your listeners to the degree that you relate it to who Jesus is and what He has done. If you are a parishioner who has grown accustom to drinking coffee in the lobby until the music set or preaching begins, try finding your seat early to read through announcement slides or find the Minister of Announcements and encourage him or her. You may find Jesus in a place you'd never thought to look. In the end, it's about looking to Jesus more than anything or anyone else for direction and motivation. What can possibly motivate us more than who He is and what He has done?

Questions for Reflection or Discussion

Read 2 Corinthians 8:1-15 and consider the following questions.

1. What do you learn about the Macedonians from their giving? What amazed Paul about

their giving?

2. What "grace" had God given to the Macedonian Christians? How did this impact their desire to give and the nature of their gift?

Read 2 Corinthians 9:1-15 and consider the following questions.

1. Why did Paul say it was unnecessary for him to write to the Corinthians about the offering for those in need in Jerusalem? Why do you think he wrote to them about it anyway?

2. What are some issues or causes you were more enthusiastic about in the past than you are now? What changed?

3. What are some reasons our participation in ministry might fall short of what we know it ought to be?

4. How do you think it made the Corinthians feel to learn that Paul bragged about their eagerness to other churches?

5. What would motivate you to serve or give eagerly and with zeal in the church?

6. What suggestions can you share that have

helped you achieve your goals in giving faithfully?

Read 1 Peter 5:1-7 and consider the following questions.

1. Do you know your church leaders well enough to know their motives for serving the church? What action steps can you take to deepen your relationship with your church leaders?
2. Do your church leaders' personal lives serve as a model for your own walk with Jesus?
3. How often do you think of heaven to inspire you to serve?

Chapter 6

God's Country

"There are two great lies that I've heard: the day you eat of the fruit of that tree, you will not surely die, and that Jesus Christ was a white, middle-class republican. And if you wanna be saved, you have to learn to be like Him."
- Derek Webb

In our home office I have a little metal safe that holds small valuables, such as passports and some old silver dollars that have been passed down a generation or two. Also in this safe are my grandfather's military service medals: a Purple Heart and a Bronze Star.

The Purple Heart is awarded to members of the armed forces who are wounded by an instrument of war in the hands of the enemy, as well as posthumously to the next of kin in the name of those who are killed in action or die of wounds received in action. The Bronze Star is the fourth-highest individual military award, the ninth highest by order of precedence in the U.S. Military, and is awarded for acts of heroism, acts of merit, or meritorious service in a combat zone.

My grandfather earned these service medals as one of 290,000 American soldiers who beat back the communists in Korea. He did not talk about his battle experiences before his death, and all of his military records were lost in a government warehouse fire many years ago. My assumption is that he earned these medals in the same moment, wounded as he acted heroically for the cause of freedom.

Papaw died when I was around 5, so my memories of him are sparse but heartwarming. Without Papaw, I wouldn't know how to harvest pecans, "rest my eyes" in the recliner, or enjoy Circus Peanuts. I have very fond memories of spending Sunday mornings with him. He picked me up early each week and took me to the Delta Motel Diner, where he had black coffee and I had a big, fat donut (and maybe a little of his coffee). Then he took me to First Baptist Church of Boyle, MS for Sunday school and "big church."

After his death, we moved our membership to First Baptist Church of Cleveland, MS, where God saved me and called me to serve the church. Just as his love for liberty led him to bravely serve his country, his love for the Lord led him to honorably serve his family. How grateful I am for Papaw and his service to God and country.

Patriotism and Piety

A love for Jesus and a love for country are one in the same for many Christians in the South. In June of 2013, the Public Religion Research Institute conducted a survey of more than a thousand Americans, asking them about their religious life and their feelings about their country. Not surprisingly, more than 80% of all participants said they were "extremely proud" or "very proud" to be an American.

Most fascinating is that white evangelicals were more likely than any other religious group surveyed to believe that God has granted the U.S. a special role in history (84 percent), while only 40% of Americans who claim no religious affiliation believed the same thing. The research director particularly stated, "A lot of evangelicals live in the South, and flying a flag from your house or car, and singing the national anthem—not just standing for it—is infused in southern life."[1]

One need only attend an Independence Day worship service in a classic Southern Baptist church to see how deeply love of God and country are intertwined. One of my most memorable worship experiences occurred in such a service. After singing one or two patriotic hymns, the congregation sat down.

The senior pastor stepped down from the stage to the end of the center aisle. At the back of the room, a retired Marine in formal dress stood at the end of the aisle and requested permission to present the colors. The pastor gave his permission, and the congregation promptly stood and turned toward the center aisle.

There was a weighty, solemn spirit in the sanctuary as the marine marched smartly down the aisle, members of the congregation turning ever so slightly back toward the front, respecting and admiring the flag. The colors were posted with great poise and care. In a firm, respectful tone, the marine called upon the congregation to salute and pledge its allegiance to the flag, which everyone did enthusiastically. Afterward, the marine returned to the back of the sanctuary in a fashion similar to his entrance, and the congregation stayed silent until they were called upon to pray and sing a hymn of gratitude to God for America.

I've had similar experiences in less traditional churches. Remember the church with the successful Christmas production? Before each performance, a band would lead the gathering crowd in worship. Energy and enthusiasm was generally strong throughout the worship time, but arguably never stronger than when all were led in the band's rendition of "God Bless the USA" by Lee Greenwood. It was easy for some to conclude that southern Christians can be more passionate about the death of someone like my grandfather than they are about the death of Jesus.

The reasons why love for God and love for America are so entangled are as complex as the tie that binds them. Broadly speaking, Christians believe that no governmental authority exists outside the sovereignty of God, so we model good citizenship by doing things like paying taxes and respecting government employees (Matthew 22:21-22, Romans 13:1-7, 1 Peter 2:17). Yet these biblical commands do not call for a passionate love of country as much as they teach how to behave as earthly citizens with heaven as one's homeland.

Some Christians may love America because the liberty this nation gives makes it easier to live as a Christian. In parts of Laos, Christian converts face eviction from their homes for choosing Christ. It is illegal for anyone under 18 to attend any kind of religious service in China. In northern Nigeria, Christians are hunted and killed by Islamic militant extremists.[2] Not so in America.

God has sovereignly shed His common grace on the United States, giving believers an earthly citizenship that permits and encourages them to enjoy their heavenly citizenship. We can treasure freedom in America because it allows us to live freely in wait for what C.S. Lewis called their "true country."

I must take care, on the one hand, never to despise, or to be unthankful for, these earthly blessings, and on the other, never to mistake them for the something else of which they are only a kind of copy, or echo, or mirage. I must keep alive in myself the desire for my true country, which I shall not find till after death; I must never let it get snowed under or turned aside; I must make it the main object of life to press on to that country and to help others to do the same. [3]

Certainly one's interpretation of our nation's founding plays a role. Many southern evangelicals believe that the vast majority of our nation's founders were orthodox Christians who desired to build a Christian nation. A closer examination of the beliefs of people like Benjamin Franklin, Thomas Jefferson, John Adams, and George Washington reveal men who were deeply religious and virtuous, but not distinctly Christian. Stephen Nichols affirms this in his book, "Jesus: Made in America."

A secular state simply would not suffice for the founders, not only due to their personal convictions but also due to their sense of a need for a just system of law and ethics, their acute sense of one's duty to the world. But neither could the founders countenance Christ. Civil religion provided a way through the impasse. Franklin's plundering of the Puritans for a work ethic, a useful virtue, a generic God and a convenient doctrine of providence, while discarding the core and essence of their theology, represents the dynamic well. Franklin liberated Puritan energies from Purity doom, thus creating the distinctive 'American Religion.' There was a necessary place for religion and even for Christ in the new republic, just not the Christ of the Puritans, of orthodoxy and of the Bible.[4]

Regardless of one's interpretation of our founding father's doctrine and motives, the presence of Christian virtues in our nation's founding fathers at least partially explains why many evangelicals deeply love their country and proudly express their love for it.

The Bible teaches us to care about our country. Liberty makes it easier to be Christian, and our founding fathers, at a minimum, espoused virtues consistent with the Christian faith so that Christians have a vested interest in loving and supporting their country. I strongly resonate with all of these ideas. I am deeply grateful to God for my country. He put me here, and I am blessed. I love liberty, and I espouse the same virtues of our founding fathers. But what I must not do is idolize that liberty or those virtues. It is far too easy for Christians to love liberty more than Jesus and to espouse the virtues of our faith more than the God our faith is in.

Nowhere is this more a problem than in the South, where greater concentrations of evangelicals and patriots reside. We fail to understand that if we primarily dig in and fight for American virtues, including liberty, we communicate that Jesus is less valuable than a free and virtuous America. It is a form of idolatry that is both seductive and destructive. It is seductive because liberty and virtues are good things. It is destructive because it divides Christians and distorts their message.

Seduction, Division, and Distortion

Aesop was an ancient Greek storyteller who lived from 620 to 564 BC. One story attributed to him is entitled "The Four Oxen and the Lion."

A lion used to prowl about a field in which four oxen used to dwell. Many a time he tried to attack them; but whenever he came near they turned their tails to one another, so that whichever way he approached them he was met by the horns of one of them. At last, however, they fell a-quarrelling among themselves, and each went off to pasture alone in a separate corner of the field. Then the Lion attacked them one by one and soon made an end of all four.

The basic message of this fable is clear: It's easier to destroy a divided people. Both the lion and the oxen know this, yet the oxen do not believe it enough. A trivial point of disagreement became more important to them than the one thing that truly united them, their collective safety. Yet a disagreement is really nothing more than an attempt to agree on something else other than that which people already agree.

Whatever the oxen were "a-quarrelling" about is of no consequence. That they attempted to base their unity on something else other than what really mattered is what led to the disagreement and their demise. So the fable also has another lesson: Whenever a group of people who are designed to primarily unite around one thing try to unite around something else, the result is devastating for all.

We see this principle at work all throughout the New Testament. Consider the church at Corinth. Some members declared themselves followers of the Apostle Paul who planted the church. Others followed Apollos, a gifted, charismatic preacher and teacher (1 Corinthians 1:10-17; 3:1-9). Others came, and came early, because of the weekly Lord's Supper parties (1 Corinthians 11:17-34).

In rebuking them at each of these points, Paul directed the Corinthians to reunite in the one Person upon whom the church is built: Jesus (1 Corinthians 1:10, 3:5, 11:23-26). He did this because a church that tries to unite around something else—even something good like founding pastors, great preaching and popular ministries—eventually collapses from a weak foundation.

Whenever New Testament authors wrote to other churches about the importance of unity, they only appealed to the person of Jesus. Paul urged local churches in and around the city of Ephesus to "diligently keep the unity of the Spirit … (for) there is one body and one Spirit – just as you were called to one hope at your calling – one Lord, one faith, one baptism, one God and Father of all, who is above all and through all and in all" (Ephesians 4:3-6). He reminded the Galatians that the basis of their community was their faith in Christ, not whether they were "Jew or Greek, slave or free, male or female" (Galatians 3:28). In describing heavenly worship, John recorded that the saints "from every tribe and language and people and nation" joined with angels and elders to praise and worship Jesus (Revelation 5:8-14).

Jesus affirmed the importance of Christian unity in Him in His prayer in John 17:20-24.

> *I pray not only for these, but also for those who believe in Me through their message. May they all be one, as You, Father, are in Me and I am in You. May they also be one in Us, so the world may believe You sent Me. I have given them the glory You have given Me. May they be one as We are one. I am in them and You are in Me. May they be made completely one, so the world may know You have sent Me and have loved them as You have loved Me.*

We learn two very important things about Christian unity in this prayer. First, the nature of our unity proclaims the nature of God to the world. Just as

God is in Jesus and Jesus is in God, so must Christians be with one another. If we are united together by anything other than Jesus, our message to the world is that God is divided in Himself, which means He is not God at all. The second thing we learn is that Christian unity is an essential testimony to the integrity of the gospel message. One of the primary ways the lost come to faith is through the witness of unity in Jesus among Christians. Divided and split churches preach an ineffective message.

That the Bible says so much about Christian unity is a testimony to the fact that there are many seductive alternatives for the church to give itself to. Fewer churches will give themselves to a false doctrine, though this, too, is increasingly common. More commonly, churches drift away from the gospel as its point of unity and bind themselves according to either the means by which they share the gospel (like Vacation Bible School or a Christmas play), or the fruit of the gospel (such as moral behavior or virtues).

The latter is very seductive, for it appears to give us the fruit of the gospel without having to offend people with whole gospel message. The results, however, are devastating. If our chief rallying cry is anything other than "Christ crucified," even something good and proper like "God bless America," we distort both the nature and message of God, and also divide the church.

These Colors Don't Run

To merely suggest that one's love of country could hinder the gospel and divide Christians is an uncomfortable if not offensive idea for many of us in the South. Recognizing America's exceptionalism as a gift from God, and seeing a biblical moral ethic woven into the fabric of our country's founding, we are grateful citizens who want to display that gratitude in many places, including corporate worship.

It has likely never occurred to many of us that some individualistic or corporate expressions of patriotism could limit the efforts of Christians and the church to love our enemies or make disciples. Any idol in the church—including the god of patriotism—can divide a church. The allure of American virtue is strong enough to blind us to the truth.

More than a few in one church I served particularly struggled with this issue, and the individual struggles often manifested themselves in corporate worship. This love for American virtue was typically on display in the constant presence of the American flag on stage. When I came to the church, the flag either anchored the pulpit or stood just behind it and to the side as a backdrop every Sunday.

While my preference was to remove it for all services, I felt it wiser to at least display the flags on Sundays that led to Memorial Day, Independence Day and Veteran's Day. This did not go over well with a few. The idea that we could worship God without an American flag on the stage was unheard of to some. Indeed, a few questioned my faith because of my supposed lack of patriotic spirit. Eventually, disagreements dissipated and we enacted my proposal.

A couple of years later, after a patriotic holiday service, I put the flags away as I or others had done on prior Sundays without incident. I came to worship the following Sunday, and both the American flag and the Christian flag anchored the music stand from which I preached. Perplexed, I took them down and put them in the closet. The next

Sunday, they were back on stage. I played this game against my unknown opponent for a few weeks. I put the flags away, only to find them back on stage the next Sunday morning.

Finally, our worship director hid them where presumably only he could find them. It worked for a time. The stage was free of flags for a few months until my last Sunday. A week or two later, I received a multimedia message from the worship director: it was a picture of the American flag on stage. Someone with keys and an admirable amount of perseverance found the hidden flags and placed them on stage, and waited for my departure to do so.

In writing about this incident many months later, I received a few angry emails like the following that demonstrates how intimately connected love of God and love of country are for many in the South. I received a few angry emails like the following email that demonstrates how intimately connected love of God and love of country are for many in the South.

You CANNOT separate the two no matter how hard you try. If it were not for the flag and all the men and women that have died for our rights to worship FREELY we would not be able today to go to Church and worship.

My interpretation of this is that the love this person has for his country is so strong that he cannot conceive of any way his Christian faith can exist apart from America. In his view, the worship of God is not possible without freedom. Yet according to Jesus, freedom does not allow for the worship of God: knowing Jesus gives us freedom to worship God (John 8:32). When American Christians such as myself make freedom a prerequisite for knowing and worshipping Jesus, we soon feel we cannot worship in a church without the presence of the American flag on the stage, especially on Sundays near patriotic holidays.

I am not alone in having these kinds of experiences. Speaking at a roundtable discussion with Steve Lawson and R. C. Sproul, Pastor Mark Dever explained his experience with Capitol Hill Baptist Church in Washington, D.C.

When I was coming to the church in Washington DC, I requested the flag be left out of the sanctuary. Over a year later, an older member of the church asked me where the flag was. I said, "What flag?" She was asking where the American and Christian flags were because Memorial Day was coming up, and we needed a flag. (I explained that) when we gather in the church we're more fundamentally Christian than American ... (that) we have much more in common with the Nigerian who is in Christ than the non-Christian across the street. She was not happy and it was taken to the church leadership. I told the deacons we could leave the flag but it's a fairly new custom and in this age things are so politicized that the flag looks like a right wing political statement. We want to reach democrats too with the Gospel. After tearful discussion, we decided to keep them out of the sanctuary.[5]

Both Dever's experience and the survey I referred to earlier call attention to the increasingly common association of patriotic expression (in his case, the presence of an American flag on stage for worship) with conservative political views. It is unfortunate that the public display of love for America has become something more commonly associated with conservatism. Most Americans, regardless of their political persuasion, love their country.[6] But knowing this dynamic exists is crucial for any church's unity and evangelism efforts. We must remember that a significant part of any gathering of Christians is the expectation that God will work in the lives of unbelievers who may be present (1 Corinthians 14:25). We must be willing to let go of the freedoms we have to celebrate American freedom and take hold of the opportunity we have to share freedom in Christ with the lost.

This concept is neither new nor foreign. Following Jesus affords believers all kinds of freedoms and privileges that we must frequently choose to forego. The Apostle Paul and the Corinthian church knew this well. Called to preach the gospel, Paul had the right to earn his living from the Corinthians while preaching there (1 Corinthians 9:14). In fact, he had earned that right more than any other preacher who might have come, given that he had planted the church.

Yet Paul also recognized that taking a stipend from them might hinder the work of the gospel. "We have not made use of this right; instead we endure everything so that we will not hinder the gospel of Christ" (1 Corinthians 9:12). Paul even goes so far as to say that his reward for preaching the gospel was "to preach the gospel and offer it free of charge and not make full use of my authority in the gospel" (1 Corinthians 9:18). He then carries his point to its logical conclusion. Even though He was free in Christ and a slave to no one, he willingly chose to enslave himself to others in order that some might come to know Jesus.

To the extent we southern Christians understand we are united first and foremost in Christ, we have the freedom and the right to express pride in our great nation. Yet knowing that many such expressions can do harm to the Kingdom of God, we must be willing to give them up in order that some might come to Christ.

In the same way that Paul found it absurd for some to believe he shouldn't be paid, we may find it absurd that others find our expressions of love for American virtues offensive. It's at that moment we must join with Paul and say, "Now I (give up this right) because of the gospel, so I may become a partner in its benefits" (1 Corinthians 9:23).

God and Country

American Christians are called to be great Americans, yet not at the expense of being great believers. We must take care to be grateful for the earthly blessings of America and her virtues, yet not mistake them for the real liberty we have in Christ. We must not forsake the special grace of the Gospel for the common grace of morality.

Scripture commands that the unity of the church be found solely in Jesus. The church is unnecessarily threatened if it in any way communicates that something or someone else other than Jesus, even gifts like freedom and liberty, are more valuable. We must advocate our heavenly citizenship more than our earthly one.

We must live for a greater freedom while affirming that freedom is great. We must be willing to lay aside the freedoms following Jesus affords in order to share the freedom Jesus gave us that we could not afford. We need to celebrate the gift of our national identity in a way that showcases our eternal destiny.

The practical implications of living in this tension may not be as obvious compared to the other southern issues we've addressed. At the congregational level, living with this tension will likely result in a spectrum of varied practices according to each church's particular circumstances. Some congregations will find it best to remove any and all references to their country for fear of confusing the gospel message with love for America. Others may discover that simply removing the flags from the service will cause enough trouble, thus pointing to a lack of spiritual maturity in some of the congregation with regard to this issue. Still others may find that a simple explanation in the service that Jesus is the ultimate treasure of the church, and that the expressed love of country need not be confused for love of conservatism, will suffice.

Individually, we must ask the Spirit to search our hearts for any disobedience, regardless of whether we are ignorant or prideful. If the Spirit finds us more concerned with what is happening in our nation than what happened on the cross, then we must repent and believe the gospel more. If we are found more desirous for the latest news in the culture war than the ancient words of Scripture, then we must repent and read the Bible more.

If the Spirit finds us doubting that He directs the heart of our nation's leaders wherever He chooses (Proverbs 21:1), then we must repent and pray for our leaders more. If the Spirit discovers hatred for Americans who, in our view, wish to tear our country away from its Judeo-Christian roots, then we must repent and love our enemies more. If we find that we are content to have a moral country void of the gospel, we must repent and believe the gospel more.

The area in which this struggle most directly challenges us is evangelism and missions. We must be willing to be less American, even on our own soil, in order to reach our nation for Christ. We must truly believe that God so loved the world (John 3:16).

We must be convicted that America is not God's chosen country, but that people from **every tribe and language and people and nation are His chosen people** (Revelation 5:9). We must labor for our faith to be understood not as a Western religion, but as the only true religion.

Can we in the South truly believe in God and country, in that manner and in that order? Can we unite Sunday after Sunday as citizens of heaven?

Should God choose to shed His grace on us in this manner, we most certainly will.

Questions for Reflection or Discussion

Read Romans 13:1-7 and consider the following questions.

1. In what area of life do you feel the strongest tension between living as an American citizen and living as a citizen of God's kingdom?
2. Have you ever been in a situation where you acted in disobedience to our government out of obligation to Christ? If so, describe what the situation was like.
3. How do you think Christians feel about politics generally?
4. What are some errors Christians might make in their approach to politics?
5. What reasons does the text give for obeying and respecting authority? Which reason is the most significant to you? Why? Does this mean that as a Christian, you must agree with every decision a government official makes?
6. What might be an appropriate way to

disagree with a government official?

7. Do you find it easy or difficult to view the government as an extension of God's sovereign rule? Why?

8. How can we pay respect and honor to government officials we don't think are very worthy of honor or respect?

Reflect on or discuss the following questions.

1. In what ways, if any, do you need to be less American in order to be more Christian?

2. Do you find it easier to love someone of a different political persuasion or someone of a different spiritual bent? Why?

3. Do you view America as a mission field to reach for Jesus or as God's country to defend for Jesus?

4. In what ways is your immediate community diverse? Ethnically? Spiritually? Politically? In which of these areas do you need to expand your horizon?

5. Do you get more defensive about your country or your faith?

Chapter 7

Southern Fried Faith

The truth does not change according to our ability to stomach it.
- Flannery O'Connor

Some may doubt my southern roots when they learn that I've never been to a county fair. I've never risked my life on a thrill ride that fits on an 18-wheeler, entered a farm animal into a competition, or ridden a mechanical bull, nor do I have any plans to do any of those things. But if I did go to a county fair, one thing I know I would do is enjoy the many southern fried delicacies.

I'm not referring to potatoes or even pickles, but to things like fried Hershey bars, Oreo cookies, and blocks of butter. These treats are sweet to the tongue but sour on the stomach. They are so delicious that you can't help but finish them and seek more, but they turn into lead balls in your belly and wreak intestinal havoc. Only time and liters of water can help the trials pass.

Time may tell a different tale, but neither of my grade school boys have the same affection for deep fried delights, not even for savory varieties. Recently I attempted to surprise them with an unhealthy treat for dinner: fried chicken. As I ripped into a chicken leg that dripped with greasy goodness, my boys removed all of the breading and pulled the meat from the bone. "I don't like all that crunchy stuff, Dad. It's too drippy with grease." I admit that I was simultaneously proud and disappointed. That they prefer healthier foods is great, but I hate for them to lose a crucial part of their southern heritage. If they give up fried chicken now, they may give up sweet tea and watching college football tomorrow.

The same is true with regard to our faith in the South. We need to remove the southern-fried breading around our faith and find the meat on the bone, but not in such a way that disregards the gift of southern culture. There will always be things associated with our culture to peel away because they distract us from the gospel or distort our message to a lost world. There are also things about being southern that make us who we are and are God's gifts to us to use for the expansion of His kingdom. The more we grow in our love for Jesus, the more we will see where to be more southern because it helps and less southern because it hinders.

Seriously, y'all – that's what being a Christian in the South is all about.

Notes

[1] http://publicreligion.org/research/2013/06/july-2013-prri-rns/#.Uhy7Niugl8M

[2] http://www.persecution.org/

[3] C. S. Lewis, *Mere Christianity*.

[4] Stephen J. Nichols, *Jesus: Made in America.*

[5] http://www.ligonier.org/blog/2010-ligonier-pastors-conference-round-table-discussion-v/

[6] Eight-in-ten Americans report that they are extremely (51%) or very proud (31%) to be American. See http://publicreligion.org/research/2013/06/july-2013-prri-rns/#.Uhy7Niugl8M

Made in the USA
San Bernardino, CA
21 June 2017